A TRUE BOOK

Queens and Princesses

Diana
Princess of Wales

Robin Doak

Children's Press®
An Imprint of Scholastic Inc.

Content Consultant
Mita Choudhury
Professor of History
Vassar College
Poughkeepsie, New York

Library of Congress Cataloging-in-Publication Data
Names: Doak, Robin S. (Robin Santos), author.
Title: Diana Princess of Wales / by Robin Doak.
Other titles: True book.
Description: New York : Children's Press, an imprint of Scholastic Inc., 2020. | Series: A true book |
    Includes index. | Audience: Grades 4–6. |
    Summary: "The book explains the life of Princess Diana"—Provided by publisher.
Identifiers: LCCN 2019031650 | ISBN 9780531131718 (library binding) | ISBN 9780531134313 (paperback)
Subjects: LCSH: Diana, Princess of Wales, 1961-1997—Juvenile literature. | Princesses—Great Britain—
    Biography—Juvenile literature.
Classification: LCC DA591.A45 D531333 2020 | DDC 941.085092 [B]—dc23

All rights reserved. Published in 2020 by Children's
Press, an imprint of Scholastic Inc.
Printed in North Mankato, MN, USA 113

SCHOLASTIC, CHILDREN'S PRESS, A TRUE BOOK™,
and associated logos are trademarks and/or
registered trademarks of Scholastic Inc.

Scholastic Inc., 557 Broadway, New York, NY 10012

1 2 3 4 5 6 7 8 9 10 R 29 28 27 26 25 24 23 22 21 20

Book produced by 22 MEDIAWORKS, INC.
Book design by Amelia Leon / Fabia Wargin Design

**Front cover:
Diana in Australia in 1983,
wearing the Spencer
diamond tiara.**

**Back cover:
Princess of Wales in
Southampton in 1984.**

Find the Truth

Everything you are about to read is true *except* for one of the sentences on this page.

Which one is **TRUE**?

T or F — Princess Diana's wedding dress was adorned with 10,000 pearls.

T or F — Diana had four children, two girls and two boys.

Find the answers in this book.

Contents

Diana in 1970.

The **BIG** Truth

An Unusual Princess

Diana always loved children.

Diana especially loved meeting and talking to children while working with charities.

3 The Queen of Hearts

4 After the Divorce

Diana and Mother Teresa.

Princess Di

Diana, Princess of Wales, was one of the most beloved members of Great Britain's royal family. She married Prince Charles, heir to the throne, when she was only 20 years old. The intense interest in the princess continued throughout her life, as she upended long-standing traditions of the monarchy. Beautiful, stylish, and constantly photographed, she became famous throughout the world simply as "Princess Di."

Princess Diana in 1989 on a royal visit to Hong Kong.

Diana used her influence with the public and the media to call attention to people suffering, and she worked for change around the globe. **She was a powerful voice** for AIDS patients, the homeless, and people who had been hurt by land mines. Today Diana is remembered as a devoted mother and an advocate for all those in need.

Diana was a distant cousin of eight U.S. presidents, including George Washington and Franklin D. Roosevelt.

A Young Noble

The Honorable Diana Frances Spencer was born on July 1, 1961, in Sandringham, England. Diana was the third child born in her family. The Spencers were an important family in England. Their history stretches back more than 500 years. The family tree even includes several kings.

Teenager Lady Diana sits with her pet pony, Souffle, in Scotland.

Diana as a toddler.

Early Days

From the beginning, Diana's life was different from the lives of most other English children. Diana came from a **noble** family. She was brought up as part of the British **aristocracy,** a class of people who have ruled Great Britain for hundreds of years.

As a child, Diana felt that some great **destiny** awaited her. Years later, Diana said that she always felt different from her friends.

Diana had two older sisters, named Sarah and Jane. She also had a younger brother named Charles.

The Spencer children were raised at Park House, a home owned by Queen Elizabeth II. The royal family also owned the house next door. Diana sometimes played with Princes Andrew and Edward, the queen's two youngest sons.

Diana, on the right, sits for a family photo with her father, brother, and sisters.

Diana's great-grandmother was American.

A Shy Girl

Young Diana was shy and quiet. She loved animals and had guinea pigs and a pony for pets. She filled her bedroom with dozens of stuffed animals.

Diana was very athletic, and she excelled at swimming and skiing. She loved music, singing, and dancing. She even dreamed of becoming a professional ballerina.

When Diana was seven, her parents divorced. The children stayed with their father. Diana missed her mother very much.

As a child, Diana liked to pose for photographs.

Diana's childhood nickname was "Duch," because she acted like a duchess.

Becoming a Lady

Diana's grandfather, the 7th Earl Spencer, died when she was 13. Her father, John, then became the 8th Earl Spencer. Diana and her sisters gained the title of "Lady." From then until her marriage, Diana would be known as Lady Diana Spencer, or Lady Di.

When Diana's father died in 1992, her brother, Charles, became the 9th Earl Spencer.

Diana was unhappy when her father sent her to live at a boarding school.

School Days

Diana was homeschooled as a young child. When she was nine, her father sent her to live at a **boarding school**. In the coming years, she would attend boarding schools in England and Switzerland.

Diana did not enjoy school. Soon after her 16th birthday, she finished her education. When she graduated, she was given an award for her volunteer work at a hospital.

Life in London

Diana moved to London where she shared an apartment with three friends. She loved children, so she took jobs working as a nanny, a dance teacher, and a kindergarten teacher.

In 1977, Diana was introduced to His Royal Highness Prince Charles at a hunting party. Charles was next in line to become king of Great Britain. He was dating Diana's sister Sarah, but they soon broke up.

By 1980, Diana had captured the prince's heart.

Diana with two of her kindergarten students.

The wedding day of Charles and Diana was celebrated as a national holiday.

Diana and Charles pose for the crowds on the steps of St. Paul's Cathedral.

From Lady to Princess

Diana met Charles when his parents were urging him to settle down. Heirs to the British throne were expected to marry and start a family.

When Charles would become king, his wife would be queen. It was important for him to choose the perfect bride. This woman must be from a noble family. She must have a spotless past and be graceful under pressure.

Diana seemed a perfect fit.

Into the Spotlight

In 1981, Diana and Charles announced their engagement. The public's interest in the shy young Lady Di skyrocketed. People wanted to know more about the woman who might one day be queen.

Photographers followed her day and night. They camped outside her apartment in London. They even went to the kindergarten where she worked and asked her to come outside for photos. Though Diana was sometimes frightened, she proved that she could handle the constant attention.

Diana and Charles look happy in their official engagement photo.

Diana and Charles had 27 wedding cakes at their reception.

The royal family poses together after the wedding.

A Fairy-Tale Wedding

On July 29, 1981, all eyes were on Lady Di as she arrived at St. Paul's Cathedral. About 600,000 people lined the streets of London and 750 million more watched on TV.

Diana's dress was adorned with 10,000 pearls and a 25-foot-long **train**. On her head, Diana wore a family **tiara**, or crown, decorated with diamonds.

After the wedding, Diana officially became the Princess of Wales.

Two Little Princes

Soon after the wedding, Princess Diana became pregnant. Prince William was born on June 21, 1982. William became second in line, after his father, to inherit the throne from his grandmother, Queen Elizabeth II.

Two years later, on September 15, 1984, Diana gave birth to Henry. Today he is known as Prince Harry.

Charles and Diana show off their two boys.

In 2017, Harry said of his mother, "She was quite simply the best mother in the world."

Diana enjoying her sons at an official event in 1995.

A Hands-On Parent

Diana taught her sons how to carry out their duties as princes. She took them on official trips and showed them how to greet the public. She even brought them with her to homeless shelters and **AIDS** clinics.

Diana also took her boys to amusement parks, movie theaters, and fast-food restaurants. And she was always there to share a hug or a laugh with them.

The People's Princess

Diana was young, beautiful, and full of energy. Even though she was a princess, she had a gift for putting people at ease. She enjoyed shaking hands and hugging people she met on royal visits. Before long, she was the most popular member of the royal family.

Yet life inside the palace was not easy for Diana. She had difficulty adapting to some royal routines. She had little privacy or peace.

Kensington Palace

Once they were married, Diana and Charles lived at Kensington Palace in London. Built in 1605, this London mansion has been a favorite royal home for hundreds of years. Today, Prince William lives here with his wife Kate and their three children.

Many royals were born at Kensington, including Queen Victoria (1819–1901). Visitors to the palace can tour the rooms and sunken garden.

There is an exhibit dedicated to Diana's fashions at Kensington Palace.

An Unusual Princess

Diana was a royal rebel. She sometimes broke with tradition and did things in her own unique way.

Family trip.

Tradition: Two heirs to the throne should never take the same airline flight.

Diana's Way: Diana and Charles took William on a flight with them to Australia.

Tradition: Wear a hat at most events.

Diana's Way: Diana cut down on wearing hats so that she could better hug the children she met.

No hats here.

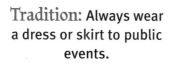

Trendsetter.

Tradition: Never talk about your problems to the media.

Diana's Way: In 1995, Diana gave an interview to a reporter to let the public know how unhappy she was.

Tradition: Always wear a dress or skirt to public events.

Diana's Way: Diana was the first royal to be seen frequently wearing pants in public.

Diana on TV.

One of the most popular modern royals, Diana was recognized around the world.

Schoolchildren cheer for Diana as she arrives to christen a new cruise ship *Royal Princess*.

The Queen of Hearts

Diana's life as a princess was a busy one. She traveled all around the world on official business and on vacation. She always tried to take her boys with her when she went on long trips.

Everywhere Diana went, people were impressed by her warmth and friendliness. She was willing to shake hands or hug those who came to see her. No matter what was going on in the princess's personal life, she had a smile for everyone she met.

A Style Superstar

Diana loved fashion. She loved to try new styles. Her designer dresses and smart hairstyles were quickly copied by women around the world. Magazines were filled with photos of the princess wearing trendy, attractive clothing.

Being a princess could be fun. Diana went to concerts and parties and became friends with many famous people. She vacationed throughout the world, skiing in Austria, sightseeing in Egypt, and cruising the Mediterranean on a yacht.

Diana dressed up for a White House dinner in 1985.

The Job of a Princess

Being a member of the British royal family is also hard work. Diana had official duties that included representing the queen at public events at home and around the world.

Diana visited military troops, opened hospitals, and attended dinners and receptions. She met with presidents, the pope, and other important officials on the queen's behalf.

Diana with members of the British Army in 1988.

As Princess of Wales, Diana wrote thousands of thank-you notes for even the smallest of gifts.

Diana serves food to children during a trip to Africa.

Helping People in Need

Diana was also expected to support a number of charities. She happily embraced this part of her job. During her marriage, the princess was involved with more than 100 causes.

The charities closest to Diana's heart helped sick children, the mentally ill, people suffering from **HIV** and AIDS, and the homeless. Her support caused the public to become more aware of people who needed help.

Putting an End to Land Mines

Diana is still remembered today for her work to ban land mines. Land mines are explosive weapons used during wars. They are buried in the ground. They are meant to explode when an enemy steps on them. Land mines that have not exploded remain in the ground long after a war has ended. Innocent people are killed or injured when they step on these hidden weapons.

In January 1997, Diana visited Angola in Africa. She met with children and adults who had been injured by land mines.

During her visit, Diana walked by a minefield wearing protective body armor.

The Fairy Tale Ends

Over the years, Diana and Charles grew apart. In 1992, the prince and princess separated.

The couple angered the queen by giving interviews to reporters. Diana talked about having depression and other mental health problems. She knew that she would never be queen of England. She said she would rather be a queen of people's hearts.

Timeline: Diana and Charles

September
Diana and Charles are first photographed together at Balmoral Castle in Scotland.

1977

1980

1981

November
Diana is working as a schoolteacher. She is introduced to Charles at a hunting party.

February 6
After meeting just 13 times, Charles proposes to Diana. They marry at St. Paul's Cathedral five months later.

Charles and Diana's divorce became final on August 28, 1996. Diana gave up the title "Her Royal Highness" but was allowed to remain Princess of Wales.

Public interest in Diana stayed strong. People wanted to know who her friends were and whom she was dating. Photographers continued to follow her, constantly taking pictures of her and her sons.

September 15
Prince Harry, Diana's second son, is born.

1982   **1984**   **1996**

June 21
Diana gives birth
to Prince William.

August 28
Diana and Charles divorce.

As a single woman, Diana tried to have a more private life.

Diana had less police protection after her marriage ended.

4

After the Divorce

Moving forward, Diana created a new life for herself as a single mother. She still lived at Kensington Palace with William and Harry. She and Charles agreed to share parenting jobs equally. They worked hard to get along with each other for the sake of their children.

The princess now had fewer royal obligations. She could focus on the things that meant the most to her: her sons and her charity work.

The Catholic Church made Princess Diana's friend, Mother Teresa, a saint in 2016.

Diana visited Mother Teresa in New York City in June 1997.

Blazing Her Own Trail

No longer a member of the royal family, Diana now had more time for herself. She announced that she would retire from public life and scaled back her official activities. The princess chose six of her favorite charities to continue supporting. These included a children's hospital and groups working to end HIV and **leprosy**. She also continued to support the English National Ballet.

A Tragic End

On August 31, 1997, Diana was on vacation in Paris, France, with a friend. The two tried to have dinner at a restaurant. But as photographers and fans gathered outside, they decided to leave.

Photographers on motorbikes chased Diana's car. Her driver tried to outrun them. He lost control of the car in a tunnel and crashed violently. Diana, her friend, and the driver were killed. The princess was 36.

This is the tunnel in Paris where Princess Diana died.

At one time, the pile of flowers and other items honoring Diana outside Kensington Palace was five feet tall.

The royal family was surprised at the outpouring of public grief after Diana's death.

The World Mourns

People were shocked and saddened by Diana's senseless death. Thousands of people traveled to London to lay bouquets of flowers in front of Kensington Palace. They also left letters to the princess they loved.

People stood in line for days outside St. James's Palace to sign a **book of condolences** telling the royal family how much they had loved Diana.

A Final Goodbye

On September 6, one million people lined the streets of London to say goodbye to Diana. Her casket was carried from Kensington Palace to Westminster Abbey. William and Harry walked behind, their heads bowed in grief.

Diana's body was then taken to Althorp, her family's **ancestral** estate. The People's Princess is buried on a private island that only family members can visit.

Prince Charles, Prince Harry, the Earl Spencer, Prince William, and Prince Philip watch Diana's casket pass by.

Keeping Diana's Memory Alive

Princess Diana's **legacy** is carried on through her sons. Princes William and Harry are now grown, and they have married and started their own families. They use their mother's example to help them raise their own children.

The princes are also active in supporting charitable causes. Among these are mental health awareness.

Diana's famous sapphire and diamond engagement ring is now worn by her daughter-in-law Kate, William's wife (right).

Princes William and Harry were touched by the tributes left by the public on the 20th anniversary of their mother's passing.

In 2017, Prince William said, "There's not many days that go by that I don't think of her."

A Time to Remember

The year 2017 marked the 20th anniversary of Diana's death. People around the world paid tribute to the beautiful princess.

Diana's life did not turn out to be the fairy tale that many expected when she wed the Prince of Wales. But the good she left behind is very real and its effects are still felt today.

Diana's Family Tree

John Spencer, 8th Earl Spencer, raised Diana and her siblings.
1924–1992

Frances Ruth Roche Spenc[er] Shand Kydd divorced Diana's father in 1967.
1936–2004

Charles Edward Maurice Spencer, 9th Earl Spencer, helps safeguard his sister's legacy.
1964–

The former Diana Spencer was Princess of Wales from 1981 until her death in 1997.
1961–1997

Catherine, Duchess of Cambridge, married Prince William in 2011.
1982–

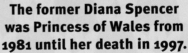

Prince William, Duke of Cambridge, is second in line to the throne of Great Britain.
1982–

Prince Philip II, Duke of Edinburgh, married Queen Elizabeth II in 1947.

1921–

Queen Elizabeth II became queen of Great Britain in 1952.

1926–

1957–

Cynthia Jane Spencer Fellowes, Baroness Fellowes

1955–

Lady Elizabeth Sarah Lavinia Spencer McCorquodale

1948–

Prince Charles is the heir to the throne of Great Britain.

1984–

Prince Harry, Duke of Sussex, is sixth in line to the throne of Great Britain.

1981–

Meghan, Duchess of Sussex, married Prince Harry in 2018. An American actress, Meghan gave up her career once she became engaged to Prince Harry.

True Statistics

Date Diana was born: July 1, 1961

Place Diana was born: Norfolk, England

Diana's wages as a nanny: $5 an hour

Number of gems in Diana's engagement ring:
15: one sapphire and 14 diamonds

Number of different fabrics used to make Diana's wedding dress: Six

Number of titles Diana held when she was married:
Eight: Her Royal Highness The Princess of Wales and Countess of Chester, Duchess of Cornwall, Duchess of Rothesay, Countess of Carrick, Baroness of Renfrew, Lady of the Isles, Princess of Scotland

Diana's height: 5'10"

Funds raised for charity by the sale of 79 of Diana's dresses in 1997: $3.25 million

Did you find the truth?

T Princess Diana's wedding dress was adorned with 10,000 pearls.

F Diana had four children, two girls and two boys.

Resources

Further Reading

Bailey, Jacqui. *Elizabeth II's Reign: Celebrating 60 Years of Britain's History.* Danbury, CT: Franklin Watts, 2012.

Howell, Izzy. *The Royal Family: Prince Charles.* London: Wayland, 2019.

Labrecque, Ellen. *Who Was Princess Diana?* New York: Penguin Workshop, 2017.

Mattern, Joanne. *Diana, Princess of Wales.* New York: Dorling Kindersley, 2006.

Norwich, Grace. *The Real Princess Diaries.* New York: Scholastic, 2015.

Zeiger, Jennifer. *Queen Elizabeth II.* New York: Scholastic, 2015.

Other Books in the Series

 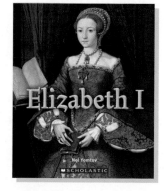 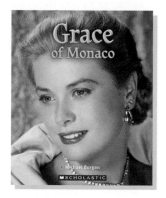

Glossary

AIDS (aydz) an illness that attacks the immune system, which protects the body against disease

ancestral (an-SES-truhl) inherited from an ancestor

aristocracy (ar-i-STAH-kruh-see) the group of people in a society who carry titles, or the most wealthy and prestigious

boarding school (BOR-ding skool) a school that students may live in during the school year

book of condolences (kuhn-DOHL-luhns-ez) a book in which people can sign their names and write their thoughts after a person's death

destiny (DES-tuh-nee) a force that is believed to control the future and the course of people's lives

HIV (h-i-v) the virus that can develop into AIDS

legacy (LEG-uh-see) something handed down from one generation to another

leprosy (LEP-ruh-see) a disease that damages nerves and flesh

noble (NOH-buhl) belonging to a family of a very high social class

tiara (tee-AHR-uh) a piece of jewelry like a small crown

train (trayn) a long, trailing piece of fabric at the back of a wedding dress

Index

Page numbers in **bold** indicate illustrations.

About the Author

Robin S. Doak has been writing for children for more than 25 years. She enjoyed researching this book by browsing through other books and the internet, looking at pictures of Diana. Robin was one of the millions of Americans who woke up early on July 29, 1981, to watch the broadcast of Charles and Diana's wedding. A graduate of the University of Connecticut, Robin lives in Maine with her husband.